4.8

Bizarre Beast Battles

T. REX VS. CROCODILE

Gareth Stevens
PUBLISHING

By Michael Sabatino

Please visit our website, www.garethstevens.com. For a free color catalog of all our high-quality books, call toll free 1-800-542-2595 or fax 1-877-542-2596.

Library of Congress Cataloging-in-Publication Data

Sabatino, Michael, author.
 T. rex vs. crocodile / Michael Sabatino.
    pages cm. — (Bizarre beast battles)
 Includes bibliographical references and index.
 ISBN 978-1-4824-2800-1 (pbk.)
 ISBN 978-1-4824-2801-8 (6 pack)
 ISBN 978-1-4824-2802-5 (library binding)
 1. Tyrannosaurus rex—Juvenile literature. 2. Crocodiles—Juvenile literature. 3. Animal behavior—Juvenile literature. 4. Animal weapons—Juvenile literature. I. Title. II. Title: Tyrannosaurus rex versus crocodile. III. Series: Bizarre beast battles.
 QE862.S3S23 2016
 567.9—dc23
                                        2015011018

First Edition

Published in 2016 by
Gareth Stevens Publishing
111 East 14th Street, Suite 349
New York, NY 10003

Copyright © 2016 Gareth Stevens Publishing

Designer: Katelyn E. Reynolds
Editor: Therese Shea

Photo credits: Cover, p. 1 (*T. rex*) Ilya Andriyanov/Shutterstock.com; cover, p. 1 (crocodile) MyLoupe/UIG/Getty Images; cover, pp. 1–24 (background texture) Apostrophe/Shutterstock.com; pp. 4–21 (*T. rex* icon) elmm/Shutterstock.com; pp. 4–21 (crocodile icon) tristan tan/Shutterstock.com; p. 4 DM7/Shutterstock.com; p. 5 Mark Hallett Paleoart/Science Source/Getty Images; p. 6 tratong/Shutterstock.com; p. 7 Ian Scott/Shutterstock.com; p. 8 elina/Shutterstock.com; p. 9 Image Source/Getty Images; p. 10 kikujungboy/Shutterstock.com; p. 11 Vijayaraghavan Sriram/Shutterstock.com; p. 12 Mark Stevenson/Stocktrek Images/Getty Images; p. 13 AndreAnita/Shutterstock.com; p. 14 Esteban De Armas/ Shutterstock.com; p. 15 Sam DCruz/Shutterstock.com; p. 16 Sergey Krasovskiy/Stocktrek Images/Getty Images; p. 17 Sergey Uryadnikov/Shutterstock.com; p. 18 Tim Boyle/Getty Images; p. 19 Orhan Cam/Shutterstock.com; p. 21 (*T. rex*) Andrew Bret Wallis/Photolibrary/Getty Images; p. 21 (crocodile) Audrey SniderBell/Shutterstock.com.

CPSIA compliance information: Batch #CS15GS: For further information contact Gareth Stevens, New York, New York at 1-800-542-2595.

CONTENTS

Words in the glossary appear in **bold** type the first time they are used in the text.

TITANIC *T. REX*

T. rex was a huge dinosaur that lived millions of years ago. *T. rex* is short for *Tyrannosaurus rex*, the dinosaur's scientific name. This **reptile** is famous for being one of the largest meat-eating dinosaurs of all time.

The mighty *T. rex* had a big mouth full of knife-sharp teeth. It hunted other dinosaurs for its meals. However, *T. rex* is thought to have been a scavenger as well. This means it fed on animals that were already dead or had been killed by another animal.

'TYRANNOSAURUS MEANS "TYRANT LIZARD" IN GREEK. REX MEANS "KING" IN LATIN. THIS "KING OF THE TYRANT LIZARDS" BECAME **EXTINCT** WITH ALL THE OTHER DINOSAURS ABOUT 65 MILLION YEARS AGO.

5

CUTTHROAT CROCODILE

Crocodiles are large meat-eating reptiles that live in the water. Their narrow body and strong tail allow them to swim quickly, chasing after fish. They also hide and wait for prey on land to wander by, then quickly attack and kill.

Modern-day crocodiles, or crocs, are very similar to their **ancestors** that roamed Earth with *T. rex* millions of years ago. Like *T. rex*, the crocodile has a large mouth full of sharp teeth it uses to tear apart its food.

CROCODILES HAVE SPECIAL BODY PARTS AROUND THEIR MOUTH THAT HELP THEM SENSE MOVEMENT IN DARK OR MUDDY WATERS.

7

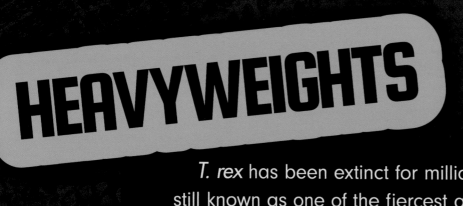

HEAVYWEIGHTS

T. rex has been extinct for millions of years, but it's still known as one of the fiercest animals ever. Let's see how *T. rex* matches up against the crocodile, one of the scariest predators alive.

LENGTH:
UP TO 40 FEET (12.2 m), FROM NOSE TO TAIL'S END

WEIGHT:
UP TO 18,000 POUNDS (8,165 kg)

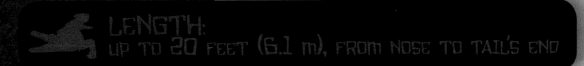

LENGTH:
UP TO 20 FEET (6.1 m), FROM NOSE TO TAIL'S END

WEIGHT:
UP TO 2,370 POUNDS (1,075 KG)

The saltwater, or estuarine, crocodile and the Nile crocodile are the two largest **species** of crocodile today.

T. rex is twice as long as the longest croc and more than seven times as heavy. It looks like the *T. rex* is the winner for both size and weight!

9

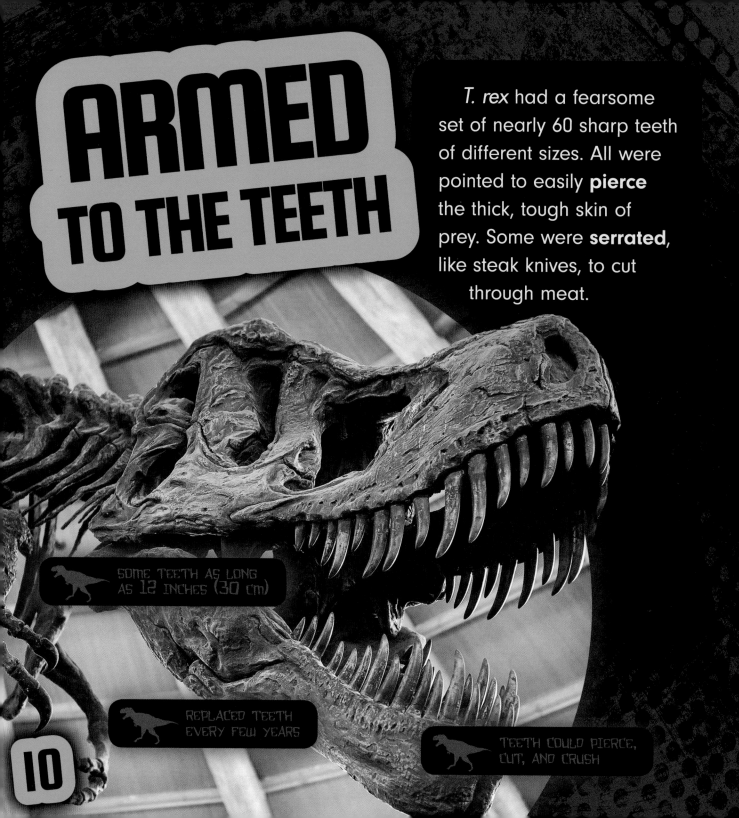

ARMED
TO THE TEETH

T. rex had a fearsome set of nearly 60 sharp teeth of different sizes. All were pointed to easily **pierce** the thick, tough skin of prey. Some were **serrated**, like steak knives, to cut through meat.

SOME TEETH AS LONG AS 12 INCHES (30 cm)

REPLACED TEETH EVERY FEW YEARS

TEETH COULD PIERCE, CUT, AND CRUSH

SOME TEETH AS LONG
AS 4 INCHES (10 cm)

CAN REPLACE EACH TOOTH
UP TO 50 TIMES

TEETH CAN SEIZE,
HOLD, AND CRUSH

Some crocodiles have more than 80 cone-shaped teeth. They use them to seize and hold on to larger prey. They can also swallow small animals whole, such as birds and fish.

A crocodile has more teeth, but *T. rex*'s chompers are definitely larger and scarier. However, prey caught by either reptile is dead meat!

13

CHEW ON THIS

As if *T. rex*'s teeth weren't scary enough, prey had to deal with the amazing power of this monster's bite—powerful enough to crush bone. *T. rex* probably had the strongest bite of any land animal ever!

BITE FORCE:
ABOUT 12,800 POUNDS (5,800 KG)

Today's saltwater crocodile has some powerful **jaws**, too. In fact, the croc has the most powerful bite of any living animal.

T. rex's bite was more than three times as powerful as the crocodile's. *T. rex* wins this battle. You still wouldn't want to be near either animal's jaws, though!

13

SPEED KILLS

Scientists have **estimated** how fast *T. rex* was able to run by looking at its **fossilized** bones. It had strong leg muscles and a powerful tail for balance. But it also had tiny arms that were probably useless in the hunt. It's a good thing *T. rex* was fast!

TOP SPEED ON LAND:
AROUND 25 MILES (40 KM) PER HOUR

TOP SPEED ON LAND:
AROUND 10.5 MILES (17 KM) PER HOUR

TOP SPEED IN WATER:
AROUND 20 MILES (32 KM) PER HOUR

Crocodiles can run pretty fast on land, but only for a short distance. A crocodile can really race in the water, though—much faster than the fastest human swimmer. Still, crocs usually **ambush** their prey.

It seems like *T. rex* would win in a land race, for sure. Scientists think *T. rex* could probably swim, too. Could it have been as fast as the speedy crocodile, though?

15

ON THE ATTACK

Most scientists agree that *T. rex* was too large to creep up on its prey without being noticed. Instead, it depended on being able to run faster than prey or on finding animals that were already dead. Scientists aren't sure whether *T. rex* hunted alone or in packs.

HUNTING METHODS:
SCAVENGING, CHASING SLOWER ANIMALS

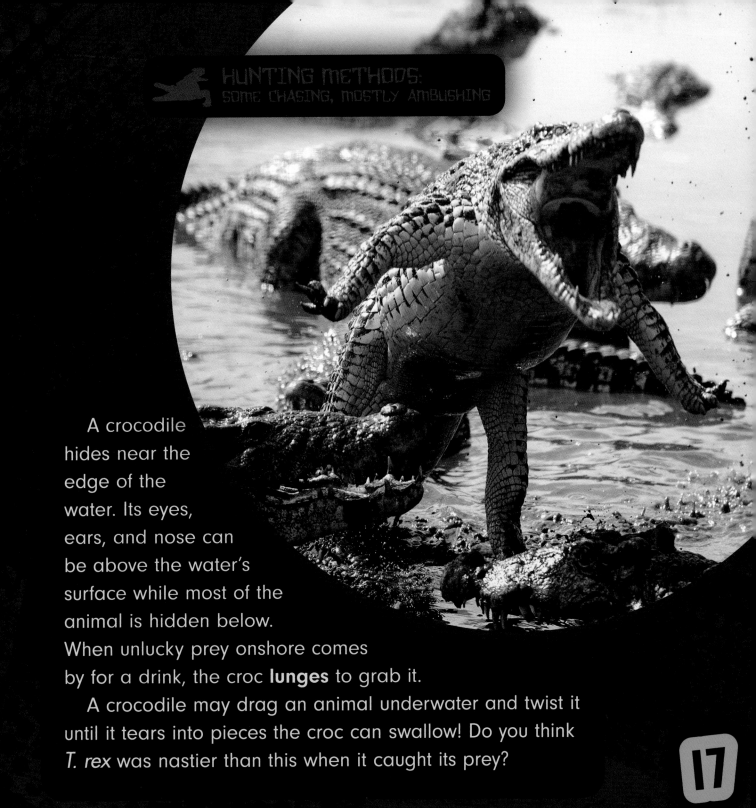

A crocodile hides near the edge of the water. Its eyes, ears, and nose can be above the water's surface while most of the animal is hidden below. When unlucky prey onshore comes by for a drink, the croc **lunges** to grab it.

A crocodile may drag an animal underwater and twist it until it tears into pieces the croc can swallow! Do you think *T. rex* was nastier than this when it caught its prey?

17

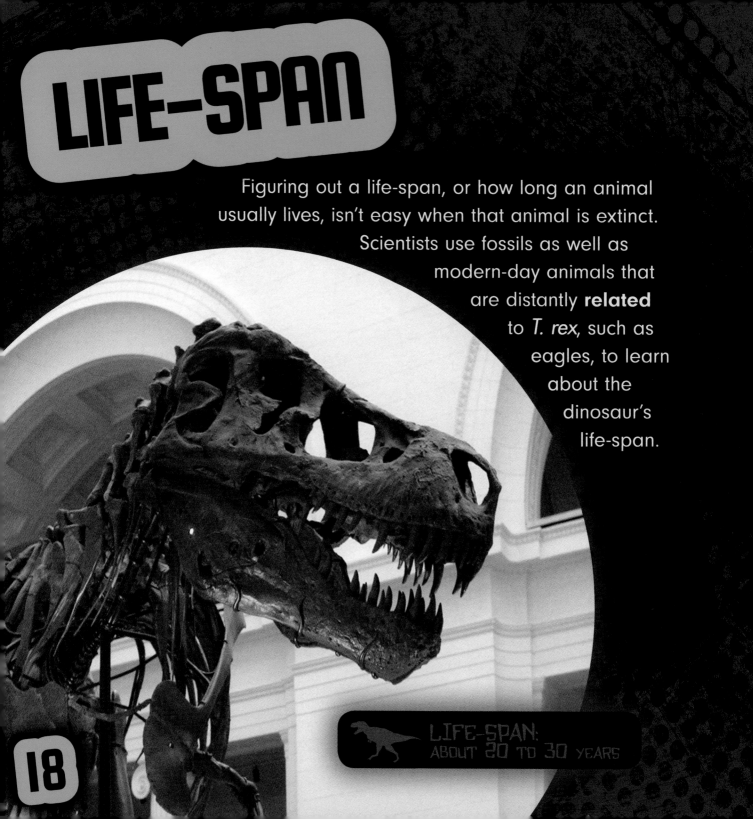

LIFE-SPAN

Figuring out a life-span, or how long an animal usually lives, isn't easy when that animal is extinct. Scientists use fossils as well as modern-day animals that are distantly **related** to *T. rex*, such as eagles, to learn about the dinosaur's life-span.

LIFE-SPAN:
ABOUT 20 TO 30 YEARS

Measuring the life-span of a crocodile in the wild is also hard, because they live so long! Scientists know that larger species, such as the saltwater crocodile, live longer than smaller species, such as the dwarf crocodile. Crocodiles win this contest. In fact, some crocs live more than twice as long as *T. rex*.

LIFE-SPAN: AS LONG AS 80 YEARS

THE WINNER?

Now that we know more about these two creatures, which would win if they battled to the death? *T. rex* is much larger than the crocodile, but the crocodile has more teeth. *T. rex* has a stronger bite, but the croc can ambush prey.

It might seem like *T. rex* wins in most areas. However, the crocodile is largely unchanged since the time of the dinosaurs. *T. rex* has been extinct for millions of years. Does that make the crocodile the real winner? You decide!

  MOST SCIENTISTS AGREE THAT *T. REX* BECAME EXTINCT 65 MILLION YEARS AGO WHEN AN ASTEROID HIT EARTH, MAKING THIS BIZARRE BEAST BATTLE IMPOSSIBLE TODAY. BUT WE CAN IMAGINE!

21

GLOSSARY

ambush: to attack from a hiding place

ancestor: an animal that lived before others in its family

asteroid: a small, rocky object in space, usually found between the orbits of Mars and Jupiter

estimate: to make a careful guess about an answer based on the known facts

extinct: no longer existing or living

fossilized: changed into a fossil, which is a hardened mark or remains of a plant or animal that formed over thousands or millions of years

jaw: the bones that hold the teeth and make up the mouth

lunge: to make a sudden forward motion

pierce: to make a hole in or through something

related: describing two animals connected by family

reptile: an animal covered with scales or plates that breathes air, has a backbone, and lays eggs, such as a turtle, snake, lizard, or crocodile

serrated: jagged or notched, like the teeth of a saw

species: a group of plants or animals that are all the same kind

FOR MORE INFORMATION

BOOKS

Bacchin, Matteo, and Marco Signore. *T. Rex and the Great Extinction*. New York, NY: Abbeville Kids, 2010.

Barr, Brady, with Kathleen Weidner Zoehfeld. *Crocodile Encounters: And More True Stories of Adventures with Animals*. Washington, DC: National Geographic, 2012.

Parker, Steve. *100 Things You Should Know About T. Rex*. Broomall, PA: Mason Crest Publishers, 2011.

WEBSITES

Dinosaur—*T. Rex*
www.kids-dinosaurs.com/dinosaur-t-rex.html
Learn about the size, diet, and habitat of *T. rex.*

Fun Crocodile Facts for Kids
www.sciencekids.co.nz/sciencefacts/animals/crocodile.html
Read more interesting facts about crocodiles.

INDEX